Glass Painting

Glass Painting
by
Emma Sedman

GUILD OF MASTER CRAFTSMAN PUBLICATIONS LTD

First published 1999 by
Guild of Master Craftsman Publications Ltd,
166 High Street, Lewes,
East Sussex BN7 1XU

ISBN 1 86108 133 2

Photographer: Graham Mathers
Editor: Andy Charman
Designer: Philip Jones at Lime Green Horse
Typeface: Book Antiqua and Gill Sans
Colour origination by Viscan Graphics (Singapore)
Printed and bound by Kyodo Printing (Singapore) under the supervision
of MRM Graphics, Winslow, Buckinghamshire, UK

10 9 8 7 6 5 4 3 2 1

To the memory of my grandmother,
Mrs Clara Elizabeth Frankish

Acknowledgements

I would to thank the following companies who have helped me with information and samples of their products: ColArt (Lefranc & Bourgeois), Whitefriars Avenue, Harrow, Middlesex HA3 5RH; Decofin, Royal Talons B.V., PO Box 4, 7300 AA Apeldoorn, Netherlands; Edding (UK) Ltd, Merlin Centre, Acrewood Way, St Albans, Herts AL4 0JY; Pébéo (UK) Ltd, 109 Solent Business Centre, Millbrook Road West, Millbrook, Southampton, SO15 0HW; and Plaid Enterprises Inc, 1649 International Court, Norcross, GA 30093 USA.

Thank you also to Peter Jones Windows Ltd of Harrogate for the window featured on page 89.

Most of all I would like to thank my family for all the support they have given me.

The publishers would like to thank Graham and Lesley Mathers for their hospitality and the superb photographs.

CONTENTS

INTRODUCTION

With glass painting you can produce stunning items of vibrantly coloured glassware in a short time and with very few materials. It's a craft which is becoming increasingly popular and the wide range of glass paints now available makes it easily accessible. It is fun and rewarding, and anyone can do it; all you need is enthusiasm and a steady hand.

You can buy inexpensive plain glassware from kitchen reject shops or even car boot sales, but before you rush out to the shops, have a look around – you'll be surprised how much potential you already have in your own home. You can turn an old wine bottle into an imaginative candleholder centrepiece for a table, and jam jars can become brightly coloured vases or tealight holders. Let your imagination run riot and have fun creating unique pieces for your home and unusual gifts for your friends. They will treasure them and you will have the satisfaction of knowing that they are originals.

Most glass and plastic surfaces can be decorated with glass paints and I can guarantee that once you're hooked there will be few remaining pieces of plain glass in your home.

GLASS PAINTING
THE BASICS

TOOLS AND MATERIALS

As glass painting increases in popularity, so glass paints are becoming available in a variety of different forms. Manufacturers are constantly experimenting and producing new products of improved quality.

Glass paints are available as either solvent-based or water-based products. The water-based paint is diluted with water, as you'd probably guessed, and you use water to clean the brushes between applications. The solvent-based paints should be used with white spirit (mineral spirit in the US) as a thinner and for cleaning brushes. It is advisable to use the solvent-based paints in a well-ventilated room or, better still, outdoors, because they can give off obnoxious fumes which build up in an unventilated environment (see the section on health and safety).

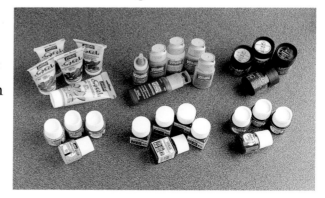

As I have already mentioned, the variety of paints available is wide. It includes products in gel form which give textured finishes, and also products that, once they have been fired in a domestic oven, can be used on items from which you eat and drink. It's important to ensure that the product you have chosen meets your particular needs. The tools and materials required for the projects are clearly listed.

Lead strip

To re-create the traditional effect of stained-glass windows, you can use lead strip to form an outline of cells which you then fill in with colour. This is available on reels in different widths and has a self-adhesive backing which makes it easy to apply.

Liquid relief liner

A popular alternative to lead strip is liquid relief liner, or outliner. It comes in a variety of colours and can be squeezed onto the glass or acetate directly from the tube. Its delicate line lends itself to intricate shapes and it hardens when it is dry to give a raised edge that you can paint up to.

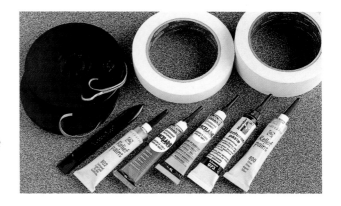

Masking or drafting tape

Another way of outlining a design is to use masking or drafting tape to block out areas of a pattern that are to remain clear. Drafting tape is slightly more expensive that masking tape, but is low tack, so it can be easily removed without leaving traces of adhesive. However, masking tape is suitable – as long as you don't leave it on the glass for too long. It is always handy to have some masking tape with you when you are glass painting, because it can also be used to hold acetate over a design that you are following, or to hold a design and carbon paper in place while you transfer the design onto your glass object.

Paintbrushes

It is also worth investing in quality paintbrushes with a good tip. These will ensure an even application of paint and will not lose bristles in your paintwork. To begin with, choose one fine, one medium and one large brush of either synthetic or sable bristles. Brushes are numbered in relation to their size – the lower the number, the smaller the head. Sizes 1, 4 and 10 are good to start with.

Palette knife

Some paints can be applied with a spatula or palette knife (see the Bowl for a Floating Candle which is painted with Pébéo Crystal Gel on page 50). A broad, flat palette knife is suitable for covering a large area.

Other useful tools

While the paint is still wet, you can use kitchen towel and cotton-buds to remove mistakes or to neaten an area where the paint may have run. For areas that prove more difficult to correct, dip the cotton-wool bud in white spirit or water first, depending on what kind of paint you are using. Be careful not to overwet the bud, however, because  this may cause the paint to run and spoil an undamaged area. You can use cocktail sticks to neaten the edges of relief liner while it is still wet.

A palette or jam jar is necessary for mixing colours and also white spirit or water for thinning and washing brushes.

Using templates

For working with the templates you need a sheet of carbon paper and a ballpoint pen, chinagraph pencil or water-based felt-tip pen , depending upon the technique you are using. For some of the projects you will also need a cutting board and a craft knife or pair of scissors, a ruler and some PVA glue. Glitter and pebbles can also be used to add decoration, and different varnishes and thinning mediums are also readily available.

The range of materials you use will depend on the projects that you are undertaking, so refer to the list at the beginning of each project before you go shopping.

Storage and care of materials

To prolong the life of your materials, it is important that you store them properly when you are not using them.

Always keep the paints in their original containers or containers that are made from the same material. Store them with the lids properly closed in a cool, dry place where there is no risk of ignition, and away from frost, heat or direct sunlight.

Replace the cap on your relief liners after you have used them, otherwise the paint may harden in the nozzle and cause a blockage. Wipe the nozzle before replacing the lid.

Always store lead strip on its original reel and do not remove the protective backing until you are ready to use it, because excessive handling or dust will reduce its adherence.

When using Pébéo Gel Crystal or Plaid® Gallery Glass® Window Color™ always store the tubes upright.

You should always wash your brushes thoroughly after use and between applications of different colours. Use white spirit or warm soapy water, depending on the paints you are using.

Health and safety

Glass painting should present no health risk if the products are used properly and according to their designation. However, always read the health and safety instructions and directions on a new product before you start using it. The following is a general guide only:

• Soak up any spills with an absorbent cloth and wash the paint away.

• Avoid getting glass paints on your skin. They may dry your skin and repeated contact could cause inflammation. Rinse thoroughly with soap and water. Do not use solvent or thinners.

• If glass paints come into contact with your eyes, flush them immediately with plenty of water and seek medical attention.

• Prolonged inhalation of solvent-based glass paints may cause headaches, dizziness, tiredness or nausea. Use them in a well-ventilated room or outdoors.

• If glass paints are swallowed they may cause stomach complaints and irritation of the digestive organs. Seek medical attention immediately.

Technical properties

Always read carefully the labels on bottles of glass paint to make sure that you are buying the ones that best suit your needs. Many glass paints are for decorative purposes only and these give beautiful rich colours in a wide spectrum. However, they are not suitable if you are looking for a paint that can be used on utility items, because they are not fully waterproof. Check the individual qualities of each range or ask for advice from the supplier.

Some glass paints can also be used on other materials, so it is worth checking this if you participate in other crafts. As glass paints improve, they are becoming more lightfast, and have better adhesion which makes them more water resistant. Some colours are more resistant to fading than others and this may also be indicated on the tube.

The drying times of different products also vary. As a general guide, most relief liners are touch-dry within an hour and colours are touch-dry within about three hours, although they may still take up to three days to dry completely. You can speed up this process with a hair dryer, but take care to use it on a low setting and at a safe distance from the object, because thin glass can crack with the heat.

It is always important to do a test with your glass paints before using them on a project. This accustoms you to the shade, spreading qualities, amount needed for good application, and drying times, before you begin on a proper piece. The painting and outlining techniques section, which begins on page 10, is designed to help you with this, but you could also make your own easy reference chart on an A4-sized sheet of acetate. Paint a small area of each different colour on the sheet and note its name and drying time next to it. This could be done with a projector pen or relief liner. Do the same for your different relief liners at the bottom of the acetate. As well as helping you to get used to the products, the chart will also enable you to choose colours which look good together.

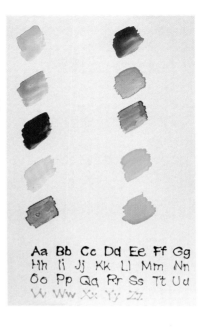

Cleaning painted glassware

Decorative painted glassware cannot be used on utility items and cannot withstand soaking or cleaning in a dishwasher unless the instructions state otherwise.

You can varnish an item to make it a little more durable and to protect it against scratches – most manufacturers include a varnish in their range – but these general guidelines should still be followed when caring for your painted glassware:

• Never place it in a dishwasher or immerse it in a bowl containing detergent.

• Do not soak or rub vigorously with a cloth.

• Varnish can also slightly improve the paint's resistance to light. If this is desired, the project should be painted in a thin coat with a large brush once the initial layer of paints has dried.

• The best way to clean your glassware is to wipe over it gently with a lukewarm, damp cloth.

TECHNIQUES

The easiest way to get to know the different glass-painting techniques is on a flat surface. You can buy sheets of acetate from craft or hobby shops. They are not expensive and they provide an ideal transparent surface on which to experiment.

The following pages demonstrate the basic techniques of glass painting and the effects that can be created. At the end of this chapter you will find instructions on how these simple practice pieces can be made into decorative greetings cards.

MASKING

This is one of the simplest ways of getting a defined edge to the paint without using relief liner. You mask out areas that are to remain transparent.

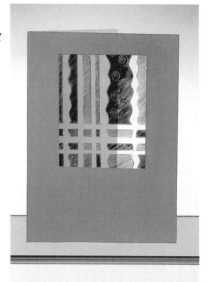

Tools and materials

Acetate sheet 100 x 80mm (4 x 3in)
Masking tape or drafting tape
Craft knife and cutting board
Transparent glass paints (blue and red)
Fine paintbrush
White spirit or water
Burnisher or pin

Method

1 Cut the acetate to size and then stick strips of masking or drafting tape onto your board. Cut them into thin strips with a craft knife, giving some wavy edges, as shown. Sticking the tape to the board helps to remove some of its tackiness, making it easier to peel off the acetate once the paint has dried.

2 Arrange the masking tape on the acetate in a pattern you are happy with. Think about the shapes you are making – all areas beneath the masking tape will remain transparent. Once you are happy with the design, press the masking tape firmly to the acetate, ensuring that all the edges are properly adhered.

3 Begin to fill in the colours. Do not overload the brush, and paint in a diagonal direction away from the edges of the tape. This helps to prevent the paint from seeping beneath it. Clean the brush well before you change to another colour and then continue.

4 Once painted, allow the acetate to dry, preferably overnight or for at least eight hours, and then remove the masking tape carefully. If the paint has bled beneath the tape in any areas you can now scrape it away carefully with the point of the burnisher or pin.

5 If there are areas you would like to enhance further, you can add interest to them by scraping shapes into the paint with a pin. Choose simple patterns, such as spirals and stars.

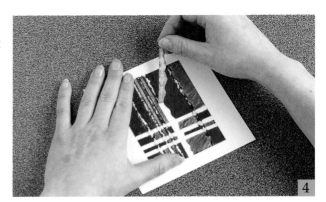

You can develop this idea further by cutting different patterns from the masking tape. From wide masking tape you can cut larger motifs, such as hearts, stars and circles.

RELIEF OUTLINING

A liquid lead outline stands proud of the surface it is on, and when it is dry it leaves an area that can be filled in with colour. This is a simple way of producing a stained-glass effect.

Tools and materials

Acetate sheet 100 x 80mm (4 x 3in)

Relief liner

Transparent glass paints (blue and green)

White spirit or water

Fine paintbrush

Method

1 Begin by applying simple wavy vertical lines to the acetate. Hold the tube of relief liner so that the nozzle is just touching the acetate and move it in a flowing line whilst squeezing gently. It takes a little practice to get used to the amount of pressure that is required to squeeze the paint from the tube evenly. Try not to be too cautious or move the liner too slowly, because this will result in an uneven distribution of paint and wobbly or broken lines. Do not allow the nozzle to become clogged, because this will make the line lumpy. While the relief liner is wet, you can wipe away smudges with a cotton-wool bud. When you have finished, leave the pattern to dry for an hour before filling in with colour. If the liner is not completely dry, it may bleed into the paint or smudge.

2 Next, fill in the colours. Do not overload the brush, but apply enough paint to give an even colour. If you have used the correct amount of paint the brushstrokes will not be visible when it is dry, because the paint settles to cover the surface smoothly. If you require a deeper colour, apply another coat of paint, but allow the first layer to dry thoroughly first. Leave the project to dry overnight.

You can stop now and leave the design as a bold pattern of intense colour, or you can decorate the surface further by drawing patterns over it with the relief liner.

3 Experiment making dots of relief liner using the tip of the tube. Apply a small amount by holding the tube vertically, squeezing and pressing the tip down onto the acetate to form a dot. Get used to making patterns with the liner and controlling the flow of paint by drawing squiggles, spirals and crosses.

4 I have used transparent paints in this exercise, but you could also try opaque colours for a different effect. These do not allow the light to pass through in the same way, and on acetate they will result in shiny blocks of colour.

Pébéo Porcelain 150 paints can be used on acetate and glass to give an opaque finish. When used on glass, they can be fired in a home oven at 150°C (300°F) to make them dishwasher resistant and safe for items that come into contact with food. Firing them in the oven also makes them more transparent. Repeating this project with both transparent and opaque stripes will show the different effects that can be created.

RELIEF LINER AS A PATTERN OR PICTURE

Once you are used to controlling the relief liner from the tube you can try creating a pattern or scene on a single-coloured background. Simple designs are the most effective for this technique and gold and silver relief liners look best on the darker coloured backgrounds, while black gives good results on paler colours. To get started, follow this exercise to make a simple aquatic scene. This will be good practice for the decanter project on page 46.

Tools and materials

Acetate sheet 100 x 80mm (4 x 3in)

Template 1 (on page 92)

Transparent glass paint (blue)

Relief liner (silver)

Large paintbrush

White spirit or water

Method

1 First, paint the acetate sheet blue, in bold strokes sweeping from left to right and working from top to bottom. You can use blue straight from the pot or mix up your own shade following the guidelines for mixing colours on page 20. On other sheets you could experiment with other ways of brushing on the paint. Allow it to dry overnight.

2 Now take the template on page 92 and photocopy it or trace it so it can be fixed behind the acetate with Blu-Tack in such a way that it does not move when you follow the design on the acetate with the relief liner. Fix it to the middle of the acetate leaving a border all round the outside. It is important to leave sufficient border if you intend to mount the picture into a card.

Trace the design onto the acetate with the silver relief liner. Work from left to right if you are right-handed and from right to left if you are left-handed. This should prevent you from smudging the areas you have just completed.

3 Once you have traced the outlines, put dots onto the fish. Allow the liner a good hour to dry before you handle the acetate. The relief liner and paints will dry more quickly with gentle heat from a hair dryer. Hold the hair dryer at least 300mm (12in) away from the acetate or glass and have it on a low setting. (This is important, because if the heat is too high it may melt the acetate or shatter the glass.)

USING TEMPLATES

1 The templates at the back of the book are easy to use on a flat surface; you simply photocopy them and place them behind the object. However unless you are painting a picture frame, most items of glassware are a little more awkward. On a curved item, such as a bowl or jam jar, that has a large enough opening, you can place the design inside and fix it with masking tape or Blu-Tack.

2 On objects that have a small opening, such as a bottle, you will need a photocopy of the template and a piece of carbon paper. Put the carbon paper face down onto the front of the glass object in the place where you want the design to be. Then put the template over the carbon paper, face up, and fix it in place with masking tape.

3 Go over the design with a coloured ballpoint pen. The pressure of the pen on the carbon paper will transfer the design onto the glass. Using a coloured line enables you to be sure that you have not missed any parts of the design. Once you have removed the carbon paper, you can follow the design with your relief liner. After the liner has dried completely, any carbon lines still visible can be removed with a little white spirit on a cotton-wool bud.

Alternatively, you can create your own templates, or draw directly onto an item of glassware using a chinagraph pencil or a water-based felt-tip pen. However, for a more complex design it is a good idea to draw it to size on a sheet of paper first. Then transfer it onto your glassware using the method just described.

ADDING GLITTER

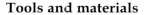

The translucent nature of transparent glass paints results in brilliant colours and effects when light passes through them. This can be further enhanced by the use of glitter. In small areas it can add an extra dimension to the pattern and the effect is increased when light reflects from the individual fragments of glitter. The following exercise uses glitter in a very simple design, but with striking results.

Tools and materials

Acetate sheet 100 x 80mm (4 x 3in)

Silver relief liner

Transparent glass paints (blue and green)

Glitter

Colourless glass paint or varnish

Fine paintbrush

White spirit or water

Method

1 First, create a grid using the silver relief liner. Do this freehand and don't worry about getting perfectly straight lines. Complete all of the lines in one direction first, and allow them to dry, before working in the opposite direction; this will prevent the point where lines meet from smudging or dragging.

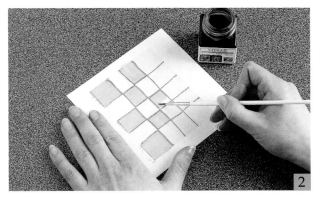

2 When the relief liner is dry, fill in the boxes with the colour that will not have the glitter – in this case the green – and allow it to dry. Add the second colour to the remaining boxes and sprinkle glitter onto these while the paint is still wet. For more control over the distribution of the glitter, apply it with your fingers rather than shaking it straight from the

tube. Allow the pattern to dry overnight and then gently dust away any glitter that has strayed from its allocated box. You can now cover the design with a colourless glass paint or varnish. This will help to seal the glitter in place.

3 You can also add colourful sequins to a project in the same way. Glass beads are also fun to use. If you wish to decorate something with beads, allow the paint to dry first and then glue the beads in position.

LEAD STRIP

Lead strip can be used instead of relief liner to define a pattern and create cells which can be filled with colour. The strips are available in different widths and can be cut to length. They also have an adhesive backing which makes them very easy to use. The lead can be quite heavy, so they are best used on glass, but for this practice project we are going to put a thin strip onto acetate. This will help you to become familiar with handling the lead, cutting joins and building up a neat pattern.

Tools and materials

Acetate sheet 100 x 80mm (4 x 3in)

3mm (⅛in) lead strip

Template 2 (on page 92)

Transparent glass paints (dark blue, light blue and light green)

Scissors or craft knife and cutting board

Boning peg

Medium paintbrush

White spirit or water

Method

1 Photocopy Template 2 or draw your own similar design on paper. (Avoid curved lines or too complicated a pattern at this stage.)

Before you use the lead strip, make sure you read the safety instructions on the packet. Lead is poisonous and you must wash your hands thoroughly after you've handled it and not eat, drink or smoke while you are working.

2 Place the acetate on top of your design and begin by making the external rectangle. The lead strip may come on a double coil and can be separated with scissors.

Cut lengths that are slightly longer than each side and angle the corners so that they make neat mitre joints without overlapping. To achieve this, cut the angles on the top strip first and, leaving the backing tape on, place it over the template. Lay one of the vertical strips in place and mark where the angle should be before making the cut. Build up the rest of the angles in this way to give neat joins that meet each other exactly. Any gaps will show once the design is painted.

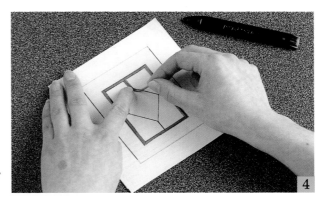

3 When you are happy with the rectangle, remove the backing tape and press the strips firmly into position. Do this one strip at a time, beginning with the top one. Press it in place and then use a boning peg to secure it. (This plastic tool comes with the lead strip packs.) First, draw the flat side of the peg over the length of the strip; then run the pointed end over the sides.

4 Build up the rest of the design by cutting lengths for each section, marking the angle before you cut the lead and then sticking it in place.

It is possible to complete a design by overlapping the lead rather than making exact joins, but this gives a heavy finish and will increase the weight on the acetate.

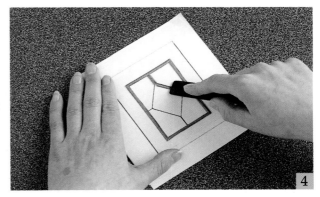

5 When all the leading is in place, paint the cells with the transparent glass paints.

This technique looks great when used on windows or doors – it looks just like stained glass. It can also be used to create a traditional diamond pattern on glass-fronted cabinets.

MIXING COLOURS

Glass paints are now available in a wonderful range of colours, and they can be mixed together to give an even greater variety of shades.

When mixing glass colours it is important to remember that solvent-based paints can only be mixed with other solvent-based paints, and the same rule of mixing like with like applies to water-based paints.

As well as mixing colours to create different shades, you can add a colourless glass paint to a coloured one to make it lighter.

Follow this exercise in mixing colours and experiment with the different shades you can make.

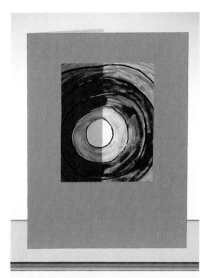

Tools and materials

Acetate sheet 100 x 80mm (4 x 3in)

Black relief liner

Transparent glass paints (red and blue)

Colourless glass paint

Palette or jam jar lid

Medium paintbrush

White spirit or water

Method

1 With the black relief liner, make a pattern of concentric circles on the acetate and allow it to dry before proceeding.

2 Use the brush to transfer some of the colourless paint to the palette. Add a small amount of red and mix them together. When mixing colours, it is important to ensure that you have made enough of the desired shade to cover the area that you are painting. It is very difficult to mix the same colour twice.

3 Use this colour to paint the inner most ring of your pattern.

4 Now add a little more red to the colour that you have already made and paint the next ring.

5 Colour the next ring with red paint direct from the pot. When the colours are dry, you will be able to see the difference between the shades you mixed and the pure colour from the pot. The pure paint will appear much deeper and look as if it has been applied more thickly.

6 For the next circle, mix a little blue with the pure red. Use this mixture with more blue added for the following ring.

7 Finally, complete the pattern by using the blue straight from the pot.

This exercise has shown how it is possible to create different shades with your basic glass colours. You can build up a collection of sample colour acetates with different colour combinations. By noting the colours you have mixed to create the different shades, you can refer to them when choosing colours for later projects.

PEELABLE PAINTS

This exercise introduces a new range of peelable paints: Plaid Gallery Glass Window Color™. What you do is paint onto special acetate leading blanks and when the design is dry, peel it off and transfer it to a window or mirror. This makes these paints ideal for creating temporary window displays for Christmas or other annual festivals, because the design can be easily removed afterwards. For larger designs, it is possible to paint directly onto the window, but using the blanks is less daunting to begin with and easier, because you are working on a flat surface.

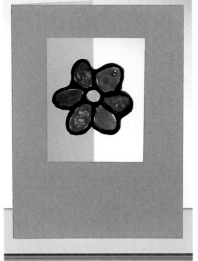

All of the colours can be applied directly from the tube via a nozzle and come as an opaque paste that, except for the black, becomes transparent when dry.

Tools and materials

Acetate sheet 100 x 80mm (4 x 3in)

Plaid leading blank

Black liquid leading

Plaid Window Colors™ (gold sparkle and royal blue)

Fine paintbrush

Cocktail stick

Water

Method

1 Use the black liquid leading to create a flower outline. You need to cut the nozzle of a new tube to allow the liquid leading to flow out of it, and the hole needs to be the right size. Begin by trimming only a small amount, because the amount you cut will determine the thickness of the line. Test on a scrap of acetate first and if the line is too thin and it is hard to squeeze the tube, make the hole a little larger. If required, use a cocktail stick to neaten off the edges of the liquid leading and ensure an even distribution of paint. Then leave it to dry.

2 Squeeze some gold sparkle into the centre of the flower. Then gently spread the paint with a paintbrush or cocktail stick and make sure that the paint reaches all of the corners; any gaps will become obvious when light shines through the design.

3 Paint alternate petals royal blue in the same way. For the remaining petals, squeeze the blue glass colour around the outer edges, and while this is still wet apply a gold strip down the centre of the petal. Use a cocktail stick to create a swirling pattern of gold and blue as shown. Allow the paints to dry for 24 hours.

4 When the paints are dry, the colours will be shiny and transparent and the whole design can be removed from the leading blank. Carefully loosen all of the edges and then slowly peel it away. The leading blank can then be re-used time and time again. You can now stick the design to most glass or acetate surfaces, as long as they are in a dry atmosphere and not prone to condensation. For this exercise, however, press the flower into the middle of your acetate so that it can be framed in a card.

GEL CRYSTAL

This new product by Pébéo comes in gel form. There are many different ways of applying it to create textured surfaces and moulded glass effects. Available in crystalline, opaline and iridescent, the range provides colours that are transparent, semi-opaque and iridescent and they can all be mixed together to produce further colours and effects.

This exercise uses the gel with a black relief liner to give a textured stained-glass effect.

Tools and materials

Acetate sheet 100 x 80mm (4 x 3in)

Black relief liner

Two crystalline colours (sapphire and antique orange)

Iridescent colour (yellow)

Medium paintbrush

Water

Palette or jam jar lid

Method

1 With the black relief liner, draw the diagonal grid on the acetate. Leave a border of about 15mm (½in) around the edge of the acetate. It is best to complete the diagonal lines in one direction first and allow them to dry for 30 minutes before doing those in the opposite direction. This will prevent the liner from dragging at the point where they meet.

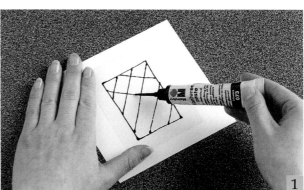

2 When the liner is dry, apply the iridescent yellow to the border. Squeeze a little into your palette and apply it thickly, using the brush in a dabbing movement. This leaves the paint thicker, with a textured surface. Do not stir the paint in the palette, because this will liquefy the gel.

3 Paint alternate diamonds with the sapphire in the same way. Clean the brush well and dab orange into the remaining diamonds.

4 To finish, add the sapphire and orange gel to the border. In some areas, dab the paint on top of the yellow gel which will now be tacky. The gel crystal needs a week to dry completely, but will be touch-dry in eight hours. Speed up the process with a hair dryer if you are impatient!

If you hold this design up to the light you can see how the diamonds have dried to look like coloured bevelled glass. By experimenting with the gel crystal you can achieve different effects. Applying it with a palette knife to larger areas will give more texture; sponging onto acetate will create a frosted-glass effect. You can also squeeze it straight from the bottle to give a colourful, thick transparent outline.

MAKING GREETINGS CARDS

These practice projects are very simple in design, but you will be surprised how effective they can look when mounted into windows to make cards.

If you have completed the projects on 100 x 80mm (4 x 3in) acetate you will find that the designs will show through windows measuring 80 x 60mm (3 x 2⅜in).

Tools and materials

A4 card (plain or coloured)
Cutting board
Craft knife
PVA glue or double-sided tape
Ruler

Method

1 You can buy inexpensive A4 card from craft shops and each sheet will make two greetings cards. First, cut a sheet in half to make two A5 pieces. Take one of these and gently score a line down the centre as shown. (Be careful not to apply too much pressure or you may cut right through the card.) This will now make a crisp foldline.

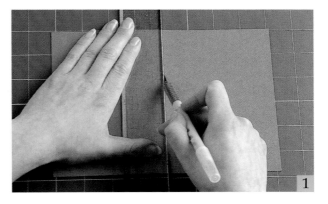

2 Turn the card over and draw a window on the right-hand side measuring 80 x 60mm (3 x 2⅜in). You can place this in the centre of the card or above centre so that the border below the design is wider than that above. Cut out the window with a craft knife.

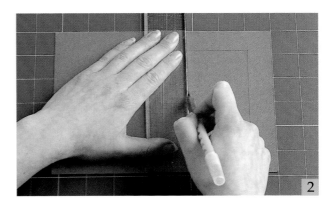

3 Now place the acetate design behind the window, painted side up, and position it so that you are happy with what you see when the card is viewed from the front.

4 Once you are satisfied with the position of the acetate, glue it in place with PVA. Do not apply too much glue – you do not want it to seep onto the front of the design. Alternatively, you can use double-sided tape to hold the acetate in place.

You shouldn't find it hard to find envelopes that will fit these cards.

Now that you have practised these simple techniques, you can make your own cards in an almost infinite variety of designs and at the same time move on to more elaborate projects with confidence.

PRACTICE PROJECTS

JAZZING UP A JAM JAR

This colourful practice project is easy to follow and uses the relief liner to transform a plain jam jar into a stylish vase. It is a good introduction to handling bulky glassware and building up confidence on a shaped surface. The simple design works well with strong colours to give a bold, brightly decorated finish.

Tools and materials

Empty jam jar
Gold relief liner
Two transparent glass paints (red and green)
Large paintbrush
White spirit or water

Method

1 Begin by cleaning the jar to ensure that it is free from grease and dust. Allow it to dry completely.

2 Make wavy vertical lines at regular intervals down the length of the jam jar using the gold relief liner. It is important that you complete an even number of lines so that the resulting bands can be painted in alternate colours.

When you are working on shaped glassware like this where you need to paint the whole surface area, you need to think before you start how best to hold the item. It may be necessary to paint it in stages, allowing areas to dry before proceeding so that you can hold the object securely without damaging the paintwork. You should allow the paint to air-dry for 24 hours before you handle it.

3 Paint the stripes on the jam jar, painting the green stripes first and then, once they're dry, the red stripes. When the main section of the jar is completely dry, paint the rim green.

4 Finish the design by squeezing dots of gold relief liner onto the red stripes and add extra wavy lines on the green areas.

You can create different effects on empty jars with the many techniques demonstrated in the previous chapter. Remember that you are working on a used jar that would otherwise have been thrown away, so don't feel constrained – work boldly with strong colours and experiment freely.

BEAUTIFYING A BOTTLE

Some wine bottles are so elegantly shaped and unusually coloured that it seems a shame to throw them away. In this practice project I show you how to use lead strip to turn a bottle into a candleholder which will brighten any room.

Tools and materials

Empty wine bottle

3mm (⅛in) lead strip

Scissors or craft knife and cutting board

Four transparent glass paints (blue, red, green and yellow)

Fine paintbrush

Templates 3a and 3b (on page 93)

Carbon paper

Ballpoint pen

White spirit or water

Method

1 Clean the wine bottle well, making sure that all labels and their adhesive have been completely removed. This is done by soaking the bottle in water and scrubbing it well with an old nailbrush. The wine bottle used here is frosted, giving an opaque background which contrasts with the transparent colours I have used.

2 Next, photocopy Templates 3a and 3b ready to transfer the design onto your bottle. Begin by cutting a sheet of carbon paper that is slightly larger than Template 3a. Place this face down in position on the bottle with the template on top of it facing up. Hold them both in place with masking tape and check that there is sufficient room for the other template 2cm (¾in) below it. This will give you a balanced composition. When you have positioned the template to your liking, go over the lines with a ballpoint pen. Press firmly so that when you remove the carbon paper the outline of the design is visible on the bottle.

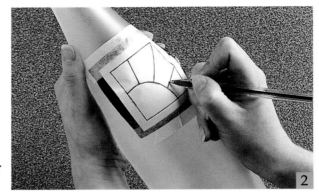

3 Repeat with Template 3b positioned below and centred with the first design.

4 Now, lay on the lead strip, starting with the bottom design. (If you begin with the top design it will be hard to avoid smudging the outline of the bottom one.)

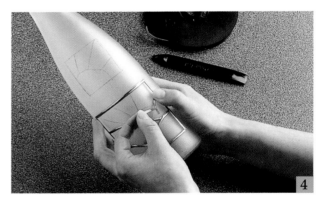

You can work out the size of the outer square, with its diagonal corner cuts, on the template first and then stick the strips to the bottle as described on pages 18–19 of the techniques section. Because the bottle presents a curved surface, the internal strips should be measured out on the bottle, as they will need to be the correct length to fit.

Cut a length of strip that is slightly longer than you need and leave the backing on it whilst you work out the shapes and where the cuts will need to be for a neat finish.

5 Remove the protective backing and secure the lead strips with the boning peg, running along each one with the concave section.

6 Secure the edges of the lead strip with the point of the boning peg.

Work with one strip at a time, holding it in position against the bottle and marking where the cut needs to be with a ballpoint pen before cutting. This will ensure that all of the joins are neat with no gaps.

7 When the lead strip is secure, begin painting the sections, cleaning your brush thoroughly between each colour. The orange was made by mixing red and yellow paint in a palette. The different shades of green were created by adding varying strengths of blue to yellow (refer to the section on mixing colours on pages 20–21 for guidance).

8 Finish the project by adding to the rim the blue that you used for the sky.

This project should have given you the confidence to use lead strip on shaped glassware. Equally stylish bottles and jars can be produced by employing the other techniques described in the techniques section which begins on page 10.

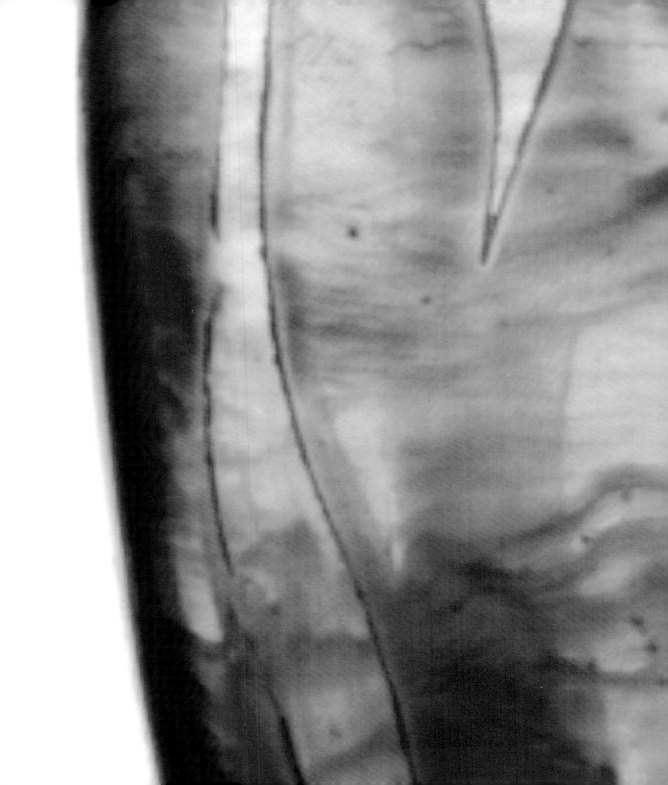

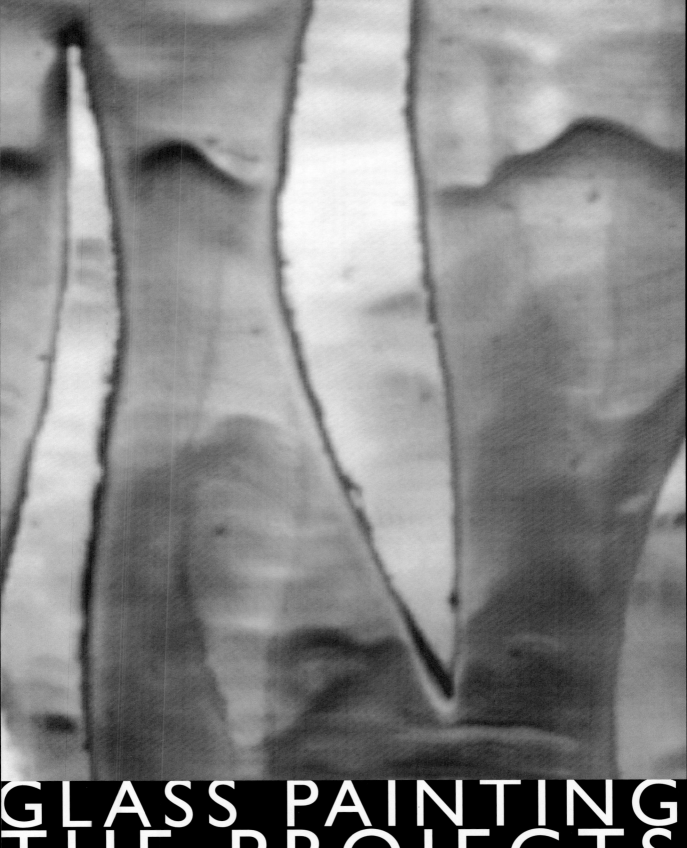

GLASS PAINTING
THE PROJECTS

RELIEF LINER AS PATTERN

Festive Candlestick

This simple candlestick is easy to make and will be an attractive addition for your festive table. Team it with a plain white or gold candle for a really eye-catching effect. You can also use the holly motif on coordinating accessories and experiment with place settings and napkin rings.

Tools and materials

Plain glass candlestick
Transparent glass paint (red)
Gold relief liner
Large paintbrush
Candle
White spirit or water

Method

1 Begin by painting the candlestick red. Painting the whole thing in one go is possible but will almost certainly result in messy fingers if not accidents with the paint! The easiest way to paint it is to hold the base first and paint from the top down, leave it for 24 hours and then hold the top to paint the base. When working in this way, try to paint down to a point where a break in the paint will not be too visible, because it may dry with a slight ridge where the two coats meet. The candlestick shown here has a raised area in the moulding, so I painted down to that first and completed the rest the following day. The break in the two separate applications of paint is not visible.

2 When the red paint is dry, use the gold relief liner to create outlines of holly leaves and berries. On an object as thin as this it is not possible to transfer the design from a template. Practise your leaves and berries on spare acetate first, or just with a pencil and paper.

Use the liner to pick out any decorative features. Here, the raised areas were defined by a band of liner.

One candlestick always looks a little lost on its own, so why not paint several in the same design? They don't all have to be the same size and dimensions – the design will bring them together. The same design on different coloured candlesticks will also look striking.

When burning candles, always remember to take sensible precautions and never leave a lit candle unattended.

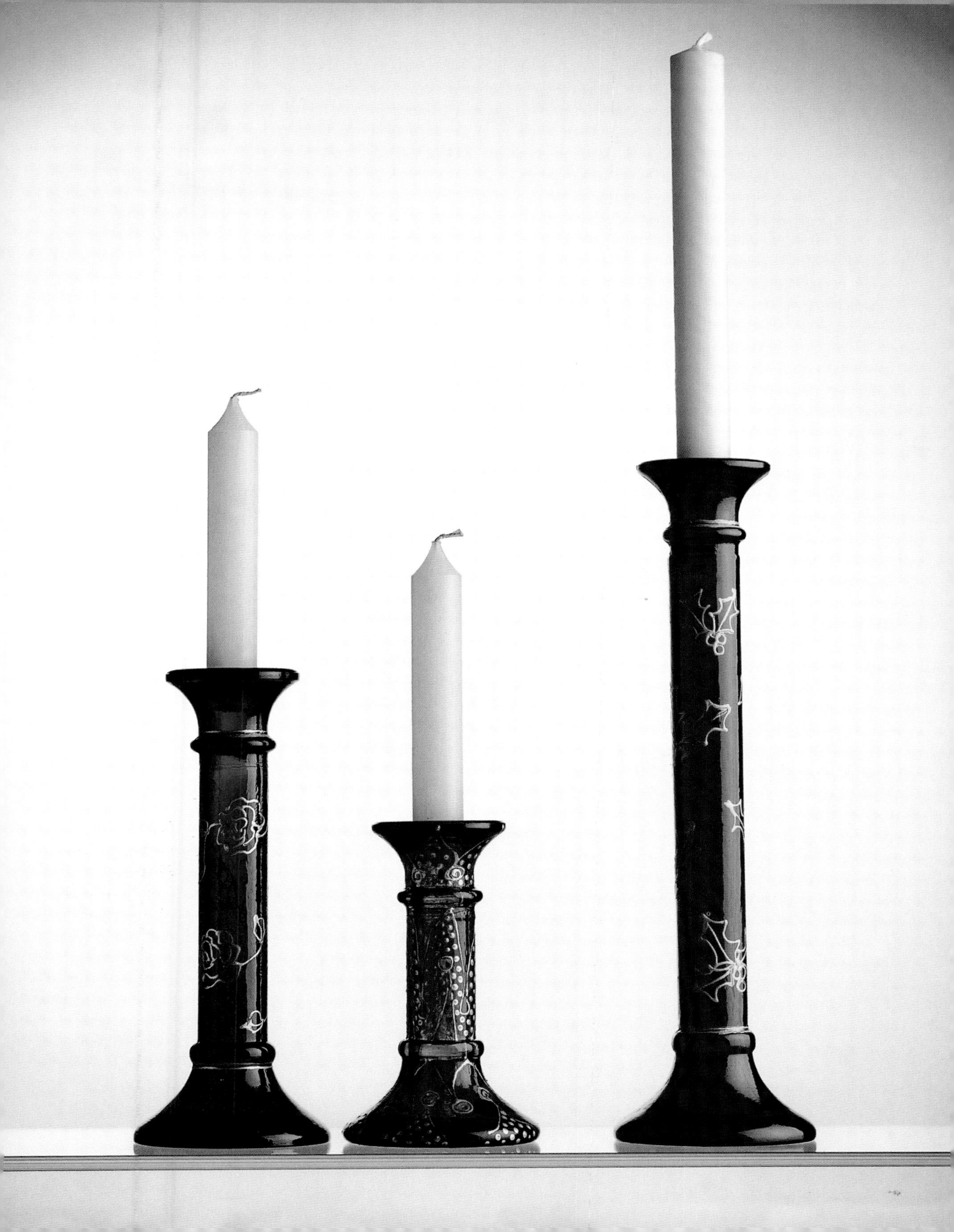

RELIEF OUTLINING

Scent Bottle

This pretty rose design transforms an undecorated scent bottle into a wonderful gift. You will find plain scent bottles in gift shops, but scent itself comes in many different-shaped bottles that will lend themselves to this treatment.

Tools and materials

Plain scent bottle
Silver relief liner
Three transparent glass paints (blue, purple and green)
Carbon paper
Ballpoint pen
Template 4 (on page 93)
Fine paintbrush

Method

1 Begin by cleaning the scent bottle thoroughly.

2 The rose design is very simple to create. It is easy to draw it freehand, but if you prefer you can trace it from Template 4. If you are going to draw it freehand, practise first on a scrap piece of acetate with the silver relief liner. Begin with a small circle in the centre and then gradually build up a pattern of petal shapes around this, making them larger as you move out from the centre. Add the leaves diagonally opposite each other as they are in the template.

3 When you are ready to decorate the scent bottle, make four equally spaced marks on the outer circumference. Begin the initial small circle of each rose at one of these marks.

4 If you are using the template to transfer the rose design, enlarge or decrease it with a photocopier according to the size of the bottle you are using. Make the four marks mentioned in step 3 and transfer the rose design onto the bottle four times using carbon paper and a ballpoint pen. Go over the design carefully with the silver relief line, making sure that you don't smudge one design while to trace another.

5

5 When the relief liner is dry, you are ready to paint the roses. On this particular scent bottle, I have painted them alternately in blue and purple, with the green of the leaves balanced by its use on the stopper.

DECORATING WITH RELIEF
LINER & MASKING

Tealight Holder

This colourful glass tealight holder actually started life as a plain dessert bowl, but it has been transformed with a little imaginative design and some brightly coloured glass paints .

Tools and materials

Plain glass dessert bowl

Masking or drafting tape

Scissors or craft knife and cutting board

Felt-tip pen

Circular stencil or large and small coin

Transparent glass paint (red)

Gold and black relief liner

Large paintbrush

Nightlight

Method

1 Begin by cleaning the bowl and leaving it to dry.

2 Stick a length of masking or drafting tape onto your cutting board. Using the circular stencil, or by drawing around a coin, mark out eight circles roughly 30mm (1¼in) in diameter. Then carefully cut them out with a craft knife or scissors. Stick them in position at different points around the glass bowl.

3 Repeat the process, this time using smaller circles roughly 15mm (½in) in diameter, and then stick these at intervals in between the large circles.

The areas under the tape will remain clear. Before you start painting, press down each circle firmly, paying particular attention to the edges of the tape, to prevent the paint from leaking under the tape.

4 Using even strokes, begin to paint the outside of the bowl; feel free to go over the tape. It may be necessary to paint the top section of the bowl first and the stem later. This will give you a dry section to hold each time and therefore better control whilst painting.

5 Leave the bowl to dry overnight and then remove the tape circles, easing the edges up with a pin to begin with.

6 Clean up any areas where the paint has bled with the edge of a craft knife or a little white spirit or water on a cotton-wool bud. Now you can begin to add the relief decoration.

To re-create the design shown here, continue by adding black dots to the centre and gold lines to the outside edges of each small circle. Decorate the large circles with an internal gold spiral and black dots around the circumference.

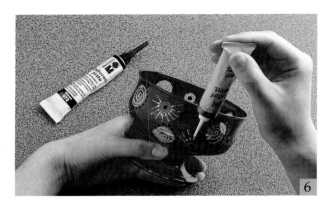

Once you are happy with the decoration, complete the transformation by adding a nightlight. Remember to always place tealight holders on a heat-resistant surface when lit and never leave them unattended, especially in a child's room.

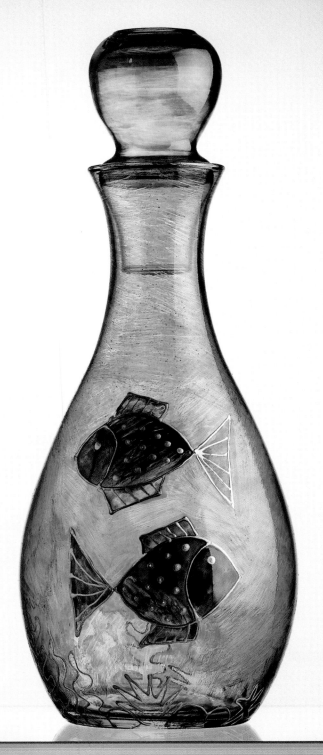

OUTLINING & DECORATING WITH
RELIEF LINER

Decanter

Decanters make elegant accessories for kitchens, dining rooms and, more unusually, bathrooms.

This decanter has been transformed with glass paints to make a fun ornament for the bathroom. Apart from looking good, it can also be used to store bath salts or bubble bath and can of course be specially designed to co-ordinate with the colour scheme or general theme of your bathroom.

Tools and materials

Plain glass decanter
Four transparent glass paints (turquoise, orange, green and yellow)
Silver relief liner
Medium and fine paintbrushes
Carbon paper
Ballpoint pen
Templates 5 and 6 (on page 94)
White spirit or water

Method

1 Thoroughly clean the decanter and leave to dry. Use Template 5 and carbon paper to transfer the fish design onto the surface.

2 Go over the design with the silver relief liner. Begin with the top fish, but hold the bottle carefully so that you do not rub off the carbon outline of the second fish with your hands.

3 Now decorate the bottom section of the decanter with pebble and seaweed shapes. Practise the sort of seabed design you want by drawing it first on a piece of paper or just take one of the designs from Template 6. Allow the relief liner to dry before you move on to the painting.

4 Paint the seaweed with shades of green and use yellow and orange for the pebbles. Use orange for the fish and the decanter stopper and leave them to dry completely. Only paint the stopper as far as the point where it meets the decanter; if you paint the whole of the stopper, the bottom section that goes inside the decanter will show through the turquoise paint when it is in place.

5 When the orange, green and yellow paints have dried, paint the rest of the decanter turquoise. Start at the base and work upwards. Use the fine brush to paint around the seaweed designs and a medium brush to cover the larger areas. When you are covering a large area like this, it is hard to complete it all before some areas begin to dry and this can cause overlap marks. Use this to your advantage by making it a feature. Here, the brushstrokes overlap along different diagonals and add depth to the paint effect. Leave the decanter to dry for 24 hours before moving on to the next step.

6 Now complete the fish by using the silver relief liner to add dots for the eyes and scales on the fins and tails.

Decanters that you intend to use for drinks should be decorated with paints that are non-toxic and water resistant, such as Pébéo porcelain paints. See the wine glass project, which begins on page 74, for details of how to use these paints.

GEL CRYSTAL & MASKING

Bowl for a Floating Candle

This bowl can be decorated simply, but to great effect, with normal glass colours and Pébéo's Gel Crystal colours. As well as being used to hold floating candles, such a container can also be designed as a fruit bowl or decorative ornament. (If you intend to use it as a fruit bowl and will be using regular glass paints, do not paint the inside, and also remember that the decoration will only withstand a light wash in cool water.)

Tools and materials

Large shallow bowl

Masking or drafting tape

Two glass paints (blue and violet)

Pébéo Gel Crystal colour (yellow iridescent)

Craft knife and cutting board

Large paintbrush

White spirit or water

Method

1 Wash and dry the bowl, then turn it upside-down and divide the base into eight equal segments using a water-based felt-tip pen or chinagraph pencil and ruler. Draw one straight, central line across the diameter and then another one at right angles to it. Add the remaining two lines between these, making sure that they go through the central point exactly.

These lines indicate where tape needs to go to create the pattern. Use either masking or drafting tape for this purpose.

2 Stick a length of tape onto your cutting board and cut it in half lengthways. This forms the stencil for the thinner clear areas. Cut the end neatly and stick it to the base of the bowl where one of your lines is marked. Secure it along to the outside edge of the bowl making sure that it is straight. Repeat for the remaining three thin strips at alternate points around the bowl.

3 Now stick thick lines of tape – the thickness it comes in – between the thin lines. Run your fingers firmly down each strip of tape to ensure that they have adhered properly and that no paint will be able to seep under the edges. Now, using the craft knife, trim the tape around the circular base of the bowl. Score the tape first, then pull away the excess.

4 Make sure that the tape is firmly in place and begin painting. Start with the base in one colour and then use this same colour in alternate segments. Next, complete the remaining segments in your second colour and allow them to dry. The drying may be speeded up with a hair dryer on a low setting. It is actually a good idea to speed up the drying, because you need to take off the tape before the adhesive becomes difficult to remove. When the first coat of paint is dry, a second may be applied if desired.

5 When the paint is dry, remove the tape and leave the bowl to air-dry overnight. At this stage you can now tidy up any area where the paint has bled beneath the tape. Use the side of the craft knife or a cotton-wool bud dipped in a little white spirit or water.

6 Use the Gel Crystal to add extra detail. Apply it with a palette knife to the whole of the outside of the bowl. This will give it a textured surface; applying it with a paintbrush will give a smoother finish. The glitter in the paint

catches the light on the painted areas and adds depth to the clear, unpainted sections.

When it is dry, fill the bowl with water and lower some floating candles into it for a striking table decoration, or take it outside to create a romantic mood for an evening barbecue.

MASKING

Vase

This vase design can be re-created with the masking method and two transparent glass paints gradually blended to give a strong tonal effect. There are many different shaped, plain glass vases available from gift shops or, alternatively, you could use old water carafes, redundant decanters that are missing their stoppers or even old jam jars as shown in the practice project on page 28.

Tools and materials

Plain glass vase
Masking or drafting tape
Cutting board and craft knife
Two transparent glass paints (red and yellow)
White spirit or water
Mixing palette
Large paintbrush

Method

1 Place strips of masking or drafting tape onto your cutting board and cut them into wavy shapes of varying lengths. Use these to create a random pattern around your vase, sticking them vertically at different heights. Remember that it is the areas that are masked that will remain clear. Make sure that the pieces of tape are not too close together, because the design will be defined by the colour and there must be plenty of it visible.

With your finger, go over the edges of each piece of tape firmly to prevent the paint from leaking beneath them.

2 The vase needs to be upside-down when you paint it and it must be supported so that the rim does not rest on your work surface. Find a suitable prop for this, such as an aerosol canister, and make sure that it is steady enough to hold the vase when both are rotated.

3 Choose your colours and a palette into which a little of each one may be poured.

You need to thin the colours for this project, so it is vital that you know whether they are water based or solvent based. To the former add water; to solvent-based paints add a little white spirit. Both colours must be of the same medium. Mix your thinner with the colour until it is a runny consistency that will spread easily over the vase. It may be a little difficult to get the balance right initially; if it is too thin, the paint will dry with runs. Test the paint on a piece of acetate held vertically over a sheet of newspaper. If the paint runs straight off it is too thin! Thin the paints very gradually, because it is easier and less costly to add more thinner than to go the other way and have to add more paint.

4 Start the painting with your lighter tone, and cover the whole of the vase quickly and evenly with a large brush. Before this has time to dry, start with your deeper shade at the upturned base of the vase. Mix lighter tones by adding thinner and yellow and gradually blend the colours as you work down the vase until you get to the light area at the bottom (really the top of the vase).

5 Once you are happy with the mix of colours you have applied to the vase, leave it to dry and then carefully peel away the tape. Clean up any areas where the paint has bled with either the edge of craft knife blade or a cotton-wool bud soaked in a little water or white spirit.

Remember to check the care instructions for the glass paints you have used before you wash the vase. Regular glass paints can only be rinsed with cold water or wiped over with a damp cloth. For a more durable finish, consider using a product such as Pébéo porcelain paint that needs to be baked in a conventional oven but results in a washable surface.

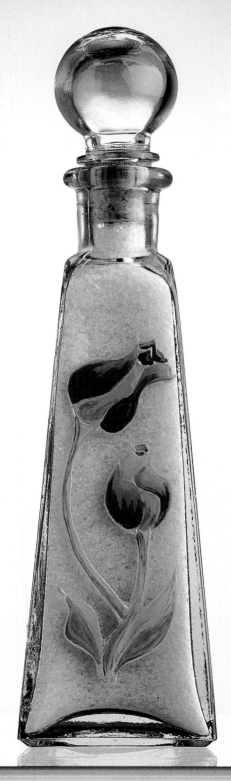

RELIEF OUTLINING &
MIXING COLOUR

Bath Salts

This decorated decanter makes a stunning container for bath salts. The glass paint has transformed a slightly predictable gift into something exciting and individual. You can also customize and colour coordinate your designs to match your bathroom or that of the person who is to receive your gift. You can buy empty decanters or corked bottles from kitchen stores and fill them with bath salts, or you can try gift shops for plain bottles that are already filled.

Tools and materials

Plain glass bottle with stopper

Template 7 (on page 95)

Bath salts, spoon and funnel (if you're filling the container yourself)

Three transparent glass paints (white, green and red)

Mixing palette

Fine paintbrush

White spirit or water

Method

1 First, ensure that the glass surface is free of dust and grease and then use Template 7 to transfer the flower design to your decanter. The decanter in the example had flat sides, therefore it was possible to place a template beneath the glass and see the design through it. For curved shapes you will need to transfer the design first using carbon paper and a ballpoint pen.

2 In a palette, mix a little of the red paint with white to make a pale pink and use this for the middle petal on both flowers. Next, add more red to make a stronger colour and paint the remaining petals. Also use this colour at the base of the first pale pink petal to add shadow. This gives an impression of depth and prevents the colour from looking flat. Continue to add shading to the remaining petals in the same way by mixing deeper pinks in the palette and using the red straight from the pot.

3 Follow the same method to paint the stem and leaves. Mix a pale green for the base colour and add shadow with some stronger shades.

4 When the design has dried you can fill the bottle with bath salts. Bath salts are available in a wide range of colours, so you can choose one which complements your bathroom or the colour scheme of your design. To minimize the mess, put the funnel into the bottle and use an old spoon to transfer the salts.

Similar bottles look good in the kitchen filled with cooking oils. You could use a different motif for each oil – a sunflower, an olive leaf, and so on.

RELIEF OUTLINING
IN SECTIONS

Lantern

Lanterns have become fashionable accessories recently and this design, which holds a single church candle, would look good in a conservatory, or as a fresh, contemporary decoration on the patio or hanging from a tree in the garden.

Tools and materials

Plain glass lantern

Grey relief liner

Three transparent glass paints (pink, orange and blue)

Fine and medium paintbrushes

Plain paper

Scissors

Carbon paper

Ballpoint pen

Ruler

White spirit or water

Candle

Method

1 Take a sheet of the plain paper and make two templates the same size as the glass panes in the lantern.

On both templates, draw a long rectangle with a border around it. In the lantern pictured, the border at the top and bottom of each pane of glass is deeper than that at the sides. The way that you structure your design will depend on the shape of the lantern and the glass area that is available. Working first on a paper template allows you to adjust and balance the design to suit your needs.

2 Now divide the rectangles you have drawn into three separate boxes, with a small gap between each one. Again, the shape of your lantern helps to determine the shape and size of your boxes. Here, the middle box has been made slightly deeper than the top and bottom ones to balance the design.

3 Once you have completed the box outlines, finish the design by drawing flowers in the boxes of one template and hearts in the boxes of the other.

4 Cut a piece of carbon paper the same size as your templates and transfer the designs to alternate sides of the lantern with the pressure from a ballpoint pen.

5 Now go over the design with relief liner, completing each section in turn.

6 When the relief liner is dry, apply the colours, using a medium brush for the larger areas and a fine one for the smaller details. It is easiest to work with the lantern on its side, but let each section dry before you turn the lantern or you might smudge what you've already painted.

7 When everything is dry, it takes only nightfall and a lighted candle to show off the full effect.

MIXING COLOURS
& ADDING GLITTER

Bookmark

This bookmark makes a simple fun project to try for yourself, or, once the outline is dry, a child may like to colour it in as an introduction to glass painting. The designs you could use on this kind of acetate-based project are almost endless.

Tools and materials

Acetate strip 50 x 210mm (2 x 8in)

Template 8 (on page 95)

Black relief liner

Four transparent glass paints (red, yellow, blue and green)

Colourless glass paint

Glitter

Fine paintbrush

White spirit or water

Method

1 Cut a strip of acetate to size and use Template 8 to follow the clown design with black relief liner.

2 When the relief liner is dry, colour in the sections with the glass paints, but leave the bow tie until all the other areas are dry. To make the orange, mix red and yellow until you achieve the strength you require and use this to decorate the selected areas. Make sure you mix enough to cover all the areas you require, because it will be very hard to mix exactly the same colour again.

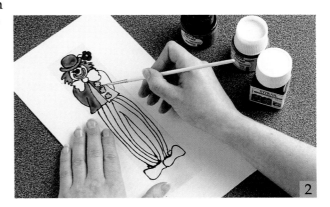

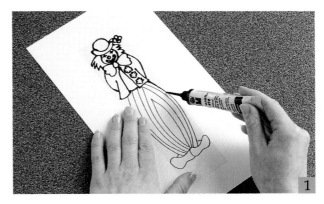

3 Leave the project to dry overnight and then use the red paint to colour the bow tie. Sprinkle glitter over this while it is wet. All of the surrounding colours are dry, so you can brush off any glitter that falls onto them. Again, allow the paint to dry overnight and then seal the glitter with a coat of colourless glass paint.

You can use the same idea on smaller pieces of acetate and decorative thread to make unusual gift tags.

LEAD STRIP
& RELIEF LINER

Mirror

This project uses the combined qualities of lead strip and relief liner to show how they can complement each other in a striking design. The lead strip gives bold outlines and defines the design while the relief liner is used to add detail. The combination of a simple design and strong colours creates a vibrant border that makes a plain mirror special.

Tools and materials

Mirror
6mm (¼in) lead strip
3mm (⅛in) lead strip
Boning peg
Three transparent glass paints (blue, turquoise and orange)
Silver relief liner
Fine paintbrush
White spirit or water

Method

1 Begin by thoroughly cleaning the surface of the mirror.

2 Cut a length of 6mm (¼in) lead strip to fit the full height of the mirror.

3 Using a water-based felt-tip pen, measure 15mm (½in) from the edge of the frame, and place the strip there. Secure the top section first and then work down the length of the strip ensuring that it is in the correct position. Once the line is straight you can press the strip firmly into place and then secure using the boning peg. Run the concave section of the peg down the length of the strip and use the tip angled on its side to run down the edges.

4 Repeat the whole process to make a second vertical strip 15mm (½in) from the other side.

5 With the two vertical strips in place, cut another section of 6mm (¼in) lead strip to fit horizontally between them 15mm (½in) from the top edge. Repeat for the bottom horizontal strip.

6 Now cut four 15mm (⁹⁄₁₆in) lengths to complete the horizontal lines on the other side of the vertical strips and make sure they are securely in place.

7 Using the 3mm (⅛in) strip, make a thinner border 10mm (⅜in) inside the one that you have just created. Angle the corners as demonstrated in the techniques section on page 18 to form neat mitred joins. Stick these strips in place.

8 With all the leading in place you can now begin to paint the border in your chosen colours. Apply the paint evenly to give a smooth finish and wash the brush well between colours.

9 Allow the paint to dry overnight and then add detail using the silver relief liner.

10 In this example, I have added swirls to the four corner squares. I marked out the wording first with a water-based felt-tip pen to get the spacing right. When you are happy with the positioning of the words, go over them with relief liner. After allowing the liner sufficient time to dry, any pen marks not covered fully by liner can be cleaned away with a damp cloth.

If you want to experiment with different designs, work on sheets of acetate cut to the right size first. You can hold the acetate over the mirror to get a good impression of what the finished piece will look like before you take the plunge and begin working on the mirror itself.

Wine Glass

Glass paints can be used to transform plain wine glasses into unique accessories that will add colour to and create a talking point for your dinner parties.

If you want the glass to be safe and durable, use Pébéo Porcelain 150 paints. It is important that you use wine glasses that are relatively sturdy, because thin glass may shatter when it becomes hot.

Glasses can be decorated for any occasion with anything from simple floral designs to words of congratulations greetings.

Tools and materials

Plain wine glass

Jam jar for testing colours

Two Pébéo Porcelain 150 paints (red and blue)

Pébéo porcelain relief liner (yellow)

Medium paintbrush

Conventional oven with heat setting of 150–160°C (300–325°F)

Baking tray and kitchen foil

Masking or drafting tape, 38mm (1½in) wide

Craft knife and cutting board

Water

Method

1 Ensure that the glass is clean.

2 The diamonds are made from masking or drafting tape. Place a strip of wide tape, tacky side down, onto the cutting board and cut eight squares with a craft knife. Carefully cut a smaller square out of the centre of each one to create a frame that can be used as a stencil. Arrange these at angles around your glass.

3 Cut from another piece of tape four hearts and four flowers to fit inside the diamonds. When you paint inside the frame, the hearts and flowers will remain clear. Bear this in mind when judging what size to make them and then arrange them on the glass. Press down firmly all areas of the tape.

4 Now you can paint the colours. To re-create the glass shown here, use red paint on the squares that contain a heart and blue on those with a flower. Brush away from the edge of the tape to avoid pushing paint beneath it. Allow the paint to dry thoroughly and then, if necessary, add a second coat.

5 At this stage, paint some yellow relief liner and red and blue paint onto an old jam jar and leave it to air-dry for 24 hours. This jar will be used to test the oven temperature and firing time before you bake your wine glass.

6 When the second coat of paint is dry, carefully remove the tape. Place a pin underneath the flowers and hearts to help raise the tape before peeling it off. Tidy up any areas where the paint has bled with the craft knife. (If you leave the masking tape in place for too long after the paint has dried, it may become difficult to remove without pulling away sections of the paint. You can avoid this by gently scoring around the edges of the tape before you remove it.)

7 Add detail to the flowers by squeezing a circle of yellow porcelain relief liner into the centre of each one. Also, add dots to the hearts.

8 Now put the test jam jar onto a baking tray covered with foil and put them into a cold oven. Set the temperature to 150°C (300°F). Once the oven has reached this temperature, time the firing for 35 minutes.

It is important that you place the glassware in a cold oven and allow it to heat up gradually. Putting a cold piece of glass into a hot oven can cause it to crack.

Check the jar after 35 minutes; the colours should have a shiny finish. If, however, they have browned slightly, it means that they have been fired for too long and the baking time should be reduced. If it hasn't been fired for long enough, they will not have glazed. Monitor it carefully and if necessary increase the temperature to 160°C (325°F). Afterwards, the jar should be left in the oven to cool down gradually.

9 Make sure that you are familiar with the nature of your oven and then bake the wine glass for the length of time indicated by your test.

Remember, it is better to underfire than overfire and ruin your colours, so don't worry about making several checks during the baking time; it can always be left in for a little longer.

If your glass has been properly glazed, it should now be safe to go in the dishwasher, but test it first with a gentle handwash and of course make sure that the original wine glass was suitable in the first place.

Now you can make your own unique set of wine glasses and extend the range with a matching decanter and tumblers.

OUTLINER GLITTER
& GLASS PEBBLES

Picture Frame

Make your own personalized picture frame for a special photograph that will really stand out! No one will believe that this started life as a humble clip frame and once you've got started the decorative possibilities are endless.

Tools and materials

Clip frame 180 x 240mm (7 x 9½in)
Three glass paints (magenta, violet and dark blue)
Colourless glass paint
Silver relief liner
Fine and medium paintbrushes
Two sheets of white card 180 x 240mm (7 x 9½in)
Silver spray paint
Glass pebbles
Silver glitter
Superglue
Cutting board and craft knife
Black felt-tip pen
White spirit or water

Method

1 First, make a card frame mount. If you have already chosen a photograph or picture, use this as a guide for the size of the mount. Cut the card to fit the clip frame and then cut a window from the centre that is the right size to frame your picture.

2 Repeat this on the second sheet of card.

3 Spray one of the mounts with the silver spray paint. Use this spray in a well-ventilated area, preferably outdoors.

4 Take the second mount and decide where you want the painted border to come. Use a black felt-tip pen and a ruler to create the grid design. Add hearts to a selection of boxes.

5 Place the glass over the design and trace it with the relief liner. First, follow the two long vertical lines. Allow them to dry and then complete the two long horizontal lines and the short horizontals. When they have dried, draw the short vertical lines. It is important to allow the lines to dry in the correct order; if they are wet they may drag. Also, if one section is already dry and you make a mistake on the next you can wipe away the mistake without spoiling what has already been completed.

Don't worry if the lines are not exactly straight; this is very hard to do freehand and anyway, slightly crooked lines add to its charm! Now draw the hearts.

6 Before you start the painting, decide where you want to put your colours and which colour will have glitter. Start painting, but leave empty the boxes that will contain glitter. Use the medium brush to paint the plain squares and the fine brush for those areas with hearts. If necessary, add a second coat after the first has dried to give a greater depth of colour.

7 Paint the boxes that are to have glitter one at a time and sprinkle the glitter onto each one while it is still wet. (If you have applied two coats to the other boxes, paint all the glitter boxes first, allow them to dry, and then proceed with a second coat and the glitter.)

When you have glittered the boxes, brush off any excess glitter with a clean, dry paintbrush and leave the project overnight to dry. Seal the glittered areas with a colourless glass paint.

8 Choose glass pebbles that will complement your frame (if you can't find the right shade, buy colourless pebbles and paint them yourself). Arrange them around the frame in a way that seems pleasing and fix them in place with a small amount of superglue.

When your frame is dry you can assemble it with the silver border you made to surround your photograph or artwork. The one shown here has a double frame to create a multi-layered look.

As an alternative to using a picture behind the glass you could paint something on top of it as shown in the photograph below. This design could match a theme in a room. You need to put plain card or paper behind it so that the wooden back of the frame is not visible.

LEAD STRIP
& GEL CRYSTAL

Bathroom Cabinet

Tidy away all those luxurious bubble-baths and shampoo bottles in this stylish, themed bathroom cabinet. The design is easy to make using lead strip and Pébéo Crystalline and Iridescent Gel Crystal to give the slightly frosted appearance.

Tools and materials

Mirror-fronted bathroom cabinet

6mm (¼in) and 3mm (⅛in) lead strip

Pébéo Crystalline Gel Crystal (sapphire)

Pébéo Iridescent Gel Crystal (yellow and silver)

Medium paintbrush

Boning peg

Template 9 (on page 96)

Carbon paper

Ballpoint pen

Scissors or craft knife and cutting board

Plain paper

String

Water

Method

1 First, cut a piece of paper to the size of the mirror on the front of your cabinet and draw a border onto it. Consider what size the rectangle in the centre needs to be in order to accommodate the shell in the centre. Once you are happy with the dimensions of your border, transfer the outline of it onto the clean mirror using carbon paper, a ruler and ballpoint pen. To transfer the shell design into the large central rectangle, use Template 9 on page 96. Enlarge or reduce it on a photocopier to the size that you require. Alternatively, you can get the shell to the size you want and design the border to fit around it.

2 The lines of the border are created in 6mm (¼in) lead strip. Start with the two long verticals first. Cut them to length and secure them with the boning peg. Now complete the horizontal lines. Begin with the longer lengths above and below the shell, then add the short horizontal strips to complete the lines.

3 Once the border is complete, use the 3mm (⅛in) lead strip to outline the shell pattern. Follow the line of the main spiral shape (line 1). To judge the length of strip required lay a piece of string along the shape first and measure that. Make a rough curve at one end of the strip and remove a small section of the backing at this end. Stick it firmly in place and then use your fingers gently to shape the lead along the curve of the line. Carefully peel the backing tape away as you bend the lead into position, running your finger over it to adhere it to the mirror as you go. When you have finished this line, cut the end with the craft knife so that it will butt up against the next piece of lead strip. It is possible to lift and readjust the lead gently before you press it down properly, but try to keep this to a minimum, because if you lift it too often the adhesive backing may lose some of its tackiness. Secure it in place with the boning peg, first over the top with the concave end then with the point along the sides.

4 Now cut a length of lead for the next layer of the shell (line 2). Begin by forming the shape roughly in your hands. Peel away a little of the backing and stick this end where it meets the lead spiral you've already done. If you need to cut the end at an angle for a snug fit, mark the angle first with a pencil and then make the cut with the craft knife. As before, gently manipulate the lead into shape with your fingers, peeling the backing away and sticking the section you are working on as you go. When you reach the opposite end, again make sure it sits neatly into the existing lead strip by marking the angle before making the cut.

5 Complete the rest of the shell outline in the same way and when you are happy that all the strips are held firmly in position you are ready to begin painting.

6 The Gel Crystal colours are thicker than regular glass paints and can be squeezed directly from the tube and then smoothed into place with a paintbrush. These paints are water based, so you can clean your brush (and daubed hands!) with water between applications. Begin by painting the shell in iridescent yellow. Squeeze a little of the colour into the first section (or onto your paintbrush) and spread it into the corners using a stippling action with your paintbrush. This will give the paint a slightly raised texture.

7 Paint the background with a mixture of iridescent silver and crystalline sapphire. The iridescent silver adds a glittered finish to the sapphire and dabbing the paint on rather than applying it with smooth brushstrokes gives the finish a frosted appearance.

8 When you have completed the background behind the shell, paint the four corners using the sapphire and silver.

8

PEELABLE PAINT

Festive Window

Children will love this fun window decoration for Christmas. It is made from special paints by Plaid that are temporary and can be removed after the festive season without damaging the glass. The nature of the paints also allows you to complete the design on special acetate 'leading blanks' and then transfer it to a window. It is much easier, and safer, to work on flat acetate than on a vertical window.

Tools and materials

Templates 10 and 11 (on pages 97 & 98)
Plaid black simulated liquid leading
Plaid Gallery Glass Window Colors (charcoal black,
*   emerald green, ruby red, royal blue and white pearl)*
Plaid leading blanks
Cocktail sticks
Water

Method

1 Practise controlling the simulated liquid leading on a scrap of acetate. As this has a larger nozzle than other relief liners, it produces a thicker line; however, you can influence the thickness by where you cut the nozzle the first time you use it.

2 When you are ready, photocopy Template 10 and place the leading blank over it with the smooth side facing up. Now, carefully follow the outline with the liquid leading. You can wipe away any mistakes or tidy the edges with a cocktail stick while the leading is still wet. Allow the leading to dry completely overnight before you begin to fill in the colours.

3 Work with each colour individually, squeezing it directly into the cells from the tube. Use the nozzle to spread the

paint to give an even application and then use a cocktail stick to work the paint into all the corners and right up against the edges of the liquid leading. This is important, because the colours must adhere to the liquid leading; even the smallest gap will be visible when the design is transferred to the window and the light passes through it.

4 Once you have applied the colours, leave the design on a flat surface to dry completely. The drying time will depend on the thickness of the paints, but it is a good idea to leave it for at least 24 hours.

5 Peel the image carefully from the leading blank. Begin by lifting one corner and then very gently loosen the area around it and peel back slowly.

6 Press the design onto the inside of a dry window or internal glass door that is not too cold or prone to condensation.

7 Use Template 11 to make the 'Merry Christmas' design. Begin with the outline of the box and the leaf, and then trace the letters. When the leading is dry, fill in the background colours, ensuring that they fuse well around all the letters.

To change or remove any of your window designs, simply peel them carefully away from the glass.

THE TEMPLATES

Template 1

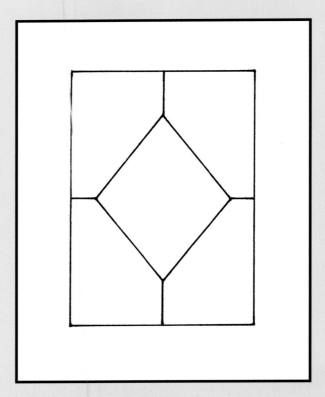

Template 2

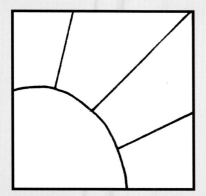

Template 3a

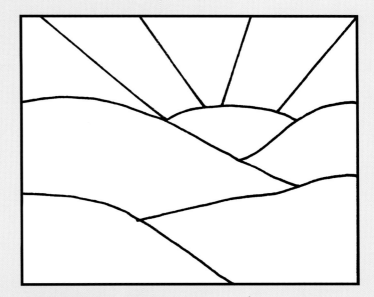

Template 3b

Template 4

Template 5

Template 6, an alternative seabed design

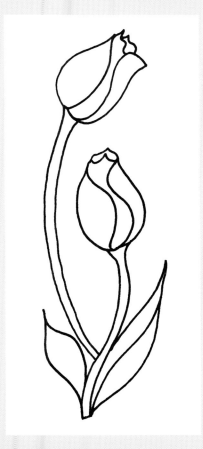

Template 7

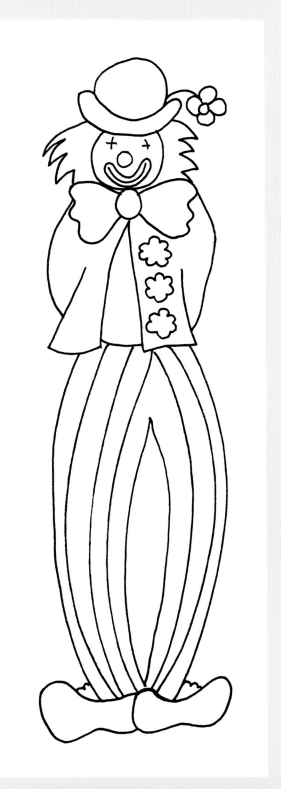

Template 8

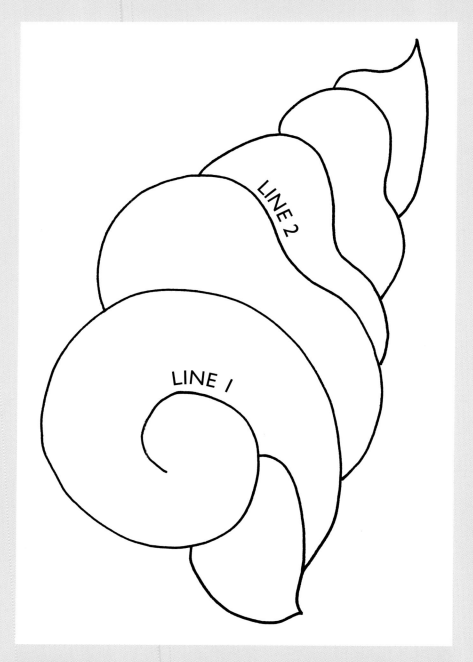

Template 9

Template 10

Template 11

ABOUT THE AUTHOR

Emma Sedman graduated in 1995 with a degree in Art & Design from the University College of Ripon and York St John. Her major subject area was jewellery design, but she specialized in enamelling and developed a fascination for colour and techniques to enhance and combine it in vibrant new forms. Emma's work was included in the 'Class of '95' exhibition at Goldsmiths Hall in London and since then she has also had a solo jewellery exhibition at Harrogate. Her interest in colour led her to experiment with glass paints, and she has been exploring their potential, on small- and large-scale pieces, for over two years. She supplies local craft shops with her work and exhibits at craft fairs.

INDEX

GMC PUBLICATIONS

Books

Woodworking

40 More Woodworking Plans & Projects
GMC Publications

Bird Boxes and Feeders for the Garden
Dave Mackenzie

Complete Woodfinishing
Ian Hosker

David Charlesworth's
Furniture-Making Techniques
David Charlesworth

Electric Woodwork
Jeremy Broun

Furniture & Cabinetmaking Projects
GMC Publications

Furniture Projects
Rod Wales

Furniture Restoration (Practical Crafts)
Kevin Jan Bonner

Furniture Restoration and Repair
for Beginners
Kevin Jan Bonner

Furniture Restoration Workshop
Kevin Jan Bonner

Green Woodwork
Mike Abbott

Making & Modifying Woodworking Tools
Jim Kingshott

Making Chairs and Tables
GMC Publications

Making Fine Furniture
Tom Darby

Making Little Boxes from Wood
John Bennett

Making Shaker Furniture
Barry Jackson

Making Woodwork Aids and Devices
Robert Wearing

Minidrill: Fifteen Projects
John Everett

Pine Furniture Projects for the Home
Dave Mackenzie

Router Magic: Jigs, Fixtures and Tricks
to Unleash your Router's Full Potential
Bill Hylton

Routing for Beginners
Anthony Bailey

The Scrollsaw: Twenty Projects
John Everett

Sharpening Pocket Reference Book
Jim Kingshott

Sharpening: The Complete Guide
Jim Kingshott

Space-Saving Furniture Projects
Dave Mackenzie

Stickmaking: A Complete Course
Andrew Jones & Clive George

Stickmaking Handbook
Andrew Jones & Clive George

Test Reports: The Router and
Furniture & Cabinetmaking
GMC Publications

Veneering: A Complete Course
Ian Hosker

Woodfinishing Handbook (Practical Crafts)
Ian Hosker

Woodworking Plans and Projects
GMC Publications

Woodworking with the Router: Professional
Router Techniques any Woodworker can Use
Bill Hylton & Fred Matlack

The Workshop
Jim Kingshott

Upholstery

Seat Weaving (Practical Crafts)
Ricky Holdstock

The Upholsterer's Pocket Reference Book
David James

Upholstery: A Complete Course
(Revised Edition)
David James

Upholstery Restoration
David James

Upholstery Techniques & Projects
David James

Toymaking

Designing & Making Wooden Toys
Terry Kelly

Fun to Make Wooden Toys & Games
Jeff & Jennie Loader

Making Board, Peg & Dice Games
Jeff & Jennie Loader

Making Wooden Toys & Games
Jeff & Jennie Loader

Restoring Rocking Horses
Clive Green & Anthony Dew

Scrollsaw Toy Projects
Ivor Carlyle

Scrollsaw Toys for All Ages
Ivor Carlyle

Wooden Toy Projects
GMC Publications

Dolls' Houses and Miniatures

Architecture for Dolls' Houses
Joyce Percival

Beginners' Guide to the Dolls' House Hobby
Jean Nisbett

The Complete Dolls' House Book
Jean Nisbett

The Dolls' House 1/24 Scale:
A Complete Introduction
Jean Nisbett

Dolls' House Accessories, Fixtures
and Fittings
Andrea Barham

Dolls' House Bathrooms: Lots of Little Loos
Patricia King

Dolls' House Fireplaces and Stoves
Patricia King

Easy to Make Dolls' House Accessories
Andrea Barham

Heraldic Miniature Knights
Peter Greenhill

Make Your Own Dolls' House Furniture
Maurice Harper

Making Dolls' House Furniture
Patricia King

Making Georgian Dolls' Houses
Derek Rowbottom

Making Miniature Gardens
Freida Gray

Making Miniature Oriental Rugs & Carpets
Meik & Ian McNaughton

Making Period Dolls' House Accessories
Andrea Barham

Making Period Dolls' House Furniture
Derek & Sheila Rowbottom

Making Tudor Dolls' Houses
Derek Rowbottom

Making Unusual Miniatures
Graham Spalding

Making Victorian Dolls' House Furniture
Patricia King

Miniature Bobbin Lace
Roz Snowden

Miniature Embroidery for the Victorian
Dolls' House
Pamela Warner

Miniature Embroidery for the Georgian
Dolls' House
Pamela Warner

Miniature Needlepoint Carpets
Janet Granger

The Secrets of the Dolls' House Makers
Jean Nisbett

GMC PUBLICATIONS

Crafts

American Patchwork Designs in Needlepoint
Melanie Tacon

A Beginners' Guide to Rubber Stamping
Brenda Hunt

Celtic Cross Stitch Designs
Carol Phillipson

Celtic Knotwork Designs
Sheila Sturrock

Celtic Knotwork Handbook
Sheila Sturrock

Collage from Seeds, Leaves and Flowers
Joan Carver

Complete Pyrography
Stephen Poole

Contemporary Smocking
Dorothea Hall

Creating Knitwear Designs
Pat Ashforth & Steve Plummer

Creative Doughcraft
Patricia Hughes

Creative Embroidery Techniques
Using Colour Through Gold
Daphne J. Ashby & Jackie Woolsey

The Creative Quilter:
Techniques and Projects
Pauline Brown

Cross Stitch Kitchen Projects
Janet Granger

Cross Stitch on Colour
Sheena Rogers

Decorative Beaded Purses
Enid Taylor

Designing and Making Cards
Glennis Gilruth

Embroidery Tips & Hints
Harold Hayes

Glass Painting
Emma Sedman

An Introduction to Crewel Embroidery
Mave Glenny

Making and Using Working Drawings
for Realistic Model Animals
Basil F. Fordham

Making Character Bears
Valerie Tyler

Making Greetings Cards for Beginners
Pat Sutherland

Making Hand-Sewn Boxes:
Techniques and Projects
Jackie Woolsey

Making Knitwear Fit
Pat Ashforth & Steve Plummer

Natural Ideas for Christmas:
Fantastic Decorations to Make
Josie Cameron-Ashcroft & Carol Cox

Needlepoint: A Foundation Course
Sandra Hardy

Pyrography Designs
Norma Gregory

Pyrography Handbook (Practical Crafts)
Stephen Poole

Ribbons and Roses
Lee Lockheed

Rubber Stamping with Other Crafts
Lynne Garner

Sponge Painting
Ann Rooney

Tassel Making for Beginners
Enid Taylor

Tatting Collage
Lindsay Rogers

Temari: A Traditional Japanese
Embroidery Technique
Margaret Ludlow

Theatre Models in Paper and Card
Robert Burgess

Wool Embroidery and Design
Lee Lockheed

Home & Garden

Bird Boxes and Feeders for the Garden
Dave Mackenzie

The Birdwatcher's Garden
Hazel & Pamela Johnson

Home Ownership: Buying and Maintaining
Nicholas Snelling

The Living Tropical Greenhouse:
Creating a Haven for Butterflies
John and Maureen Tampion

Security for the Householder:
Fitting Locks and Other Devices
E. Phillips

Videos

Drop-in and Pinstuffed Seats
David James

Stuffover Upholstery
David James

Elliptical Turning
David Springett

Woodturning Wizardry
David Springett

Turning Between Centres: The Basics
Dennis White

Turning Bowls
Dennis White

Boxes, Goblets and Screw Threads
Dennis White

Novelties and Projects
Dennis White

Classic Profiles
Dennis White

Twists and Advanced Turning
Dennis White

Sharpening the Professional Way
Jim Kingshott

Sharpening Turning & Carving Tools
Jim Kingshott

Bowl Turning
John Jordan

Hollow Turning
John Jordan

Woodturning: A Foundation Course
Keith Rowley

Carving a Figure: The Female Form
Ray Gonzalez

The Router: A Beginner's Guide
Alan Goodsell

The Scroll Saw: A Beginner's Guide
John Burke

Magazines

Woodturning

Woodcarving

Furniture & Cabinetmaking

The Dolls' House Magazine

Creative Crafts for the Home

The Router

The ScrollSaw

BusinessMatters

Water Gardening

The above represents a list of titles currently published or scheduled to be published. All are available direct from the Publishers or through bookshops, newsagents and specialist retailers. To place an order, or to obtain a complete catalogue, contact:

GMC Publications,
Castle Place, 166 High Street,
Lewes, East Sussex BN7 1XU
United Kingdom

Tel: 01273 488005
Fax: 01273 478606

Orders by credit card are accepted.

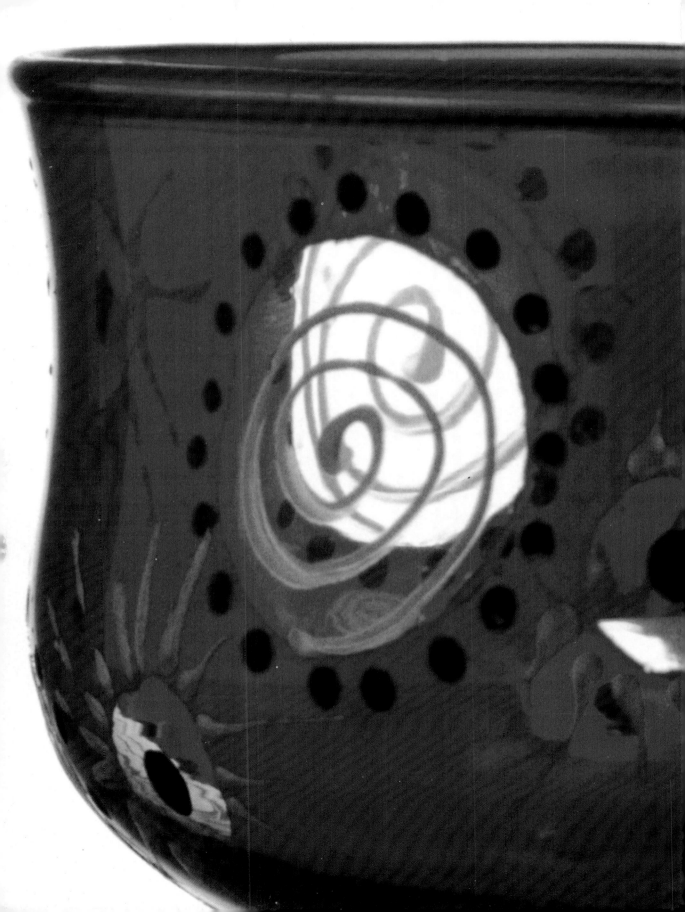